Building Leadership through Self-Insight

Taking Self-Actions that Matter

Michele Sfakianos, RN, BSN

Open Pages Publishing, LLC
P.O. Box 61048
Fort Myers, FL 33906
http://www.my411books.com/contact/open-pages-publishing
(239) 454–7700

ISBN: (sc) 978-0-9960687-4-1

Printed in the United States of America

Author/Book website: http://www.takeactionwithmichele.com

Disclaimer

The information in this book is:

- of a general nature and not intended to address the specific circumstances of any particular individual or entity;
- written as a guide and is not intended to be a comprehensive tool, but is complete, accurate, or up to date at the time of writing;
- an information tool only and not intended to be used in place of a visit, consultation, or advice of a medical professional;

This book is not intended to serve as professional or legal advice (if you need specific advice, you should always consult a suitably qualified professional.)

Dedication

. . . .

This book is dedicated to the people ready and willing to grow them-selves into a well-respected leader.

Acknowledgments

. . . .

Thank you to my team for helping me to develop this content. Thank you also to my family for their love and support through this crazy process. I hope that the late nights and weekends dedicated to the writing and research were well worth their sacrifice.

Most of all, I would like to say a big "thank you" to those that continue to support my books. Without their thirst for information and their incredible faith in me, I would not have been challenged to write. I know the hours of internet research and fact checking will help to enlighten the lives of others.

Foreword

Self-insight provides us imminent approaches that we can take to get around each corner in life. Instead of waiting for things to happen, self-insight prepares us for what is coming. Self-insight is guided by our natural instincts, which helps us to see consequences of our actions ahead of time. Thus, one builds other skills while developing self-insight, such as the ability to stay focused. In addition, one improves his or her ability to prepare and make better decisions. These skills provide you the ability to work through professional growth, which is the way to improve your job and overall life skills.

Insightfully, one can decide on what course to take before he or she jumps into any situation. For example, if you see that you need to take courses to improve your skills before applying for a better job, thus self-insight will move you to action.

For this reason, one needs to learn how to use self-insight to make good choices that helps one through professional growth. Other-wise, when the future continues into higher-grade technology, you might be one of those sitting in the waiting line of unemployment.

Central to creating a leadership footprint is:

- Defining the kind of leader you want to be. Knowing clearly how that aligns with, and helps achieve, your organizational or life vision and purpose.

- Fostering self-awareness, reflecting on your own behavior and encouraging others to give you feedback. Building relationships with others is essential.
- Developing your Self-Esteem.
- Developing your Confidence.
- Learning Stress Management and Problem Solving techniques.
- Learning about Goal Setting.
- Learning why Time Management is important.
- Choosing the assumptions about yourself and others that you need to rely on for your leadership footprint to be realistic and sustainable.

Life requires that we continue learning. Learning continuously will help one stay well versed in today's different sectors. Therefore, it is essential that we all turn inward to see what is necessary for us to advance toward the new age world.

Table of Contents

Chapter 1 - Self-Esteem

"Wanting to be someone else is a waste of the person you are."
Marilyn Monroe

Having a healthy and balanced sense of self-esteem is a major key to living a healthy and happy life. There are two sides to every coin, however. Sometimes self-esteem can become something else - namely, an unbalanced ego. So how do you know if you are simply being confident, or if you are deceiving yourself?

Healthy Self-Esteem: A healthy self-esteem is one where you have the confidence to be honest with yourself, and love yourself no matter what. A healthy self-esteem encourages you to live your life to the fullest, make bold but good choices, and to keep going if and when mistakes are made.

Low Self-Esteem: An unhealthy self-esteem goes two ways. On the one hand, an unhealthy self-esteem leaves you with zero confidence as well as an often unrelenting fear of making mistakes, and often leads to a poor quality of life.

Over-Inflated Self-Esteem: On the other hand, an over-inflated self-esteem is also unhealthy. This is a form of self-deception that tricks you into thinking that you are better than everyone else and that you can do anything, even to the point of ostracizing your friends and family.

The Dangers of Unbalanced Self-Esteem: Either way, an unbalanced sense of self-esteem can lower your quality of life. People with low self-esteem often miss out on some of the best things that life has to offer. Either they are too afraid to make a mistake, or they feel that they are not worthy of happiness. It's a type of existence that only holds you back.

An over-inflated sense of self-esteem puts you in danger of losing friends and close relationships. Outwardly, people with an over-inflated sense of self-esteem come off as cocky or mean. They tend to have trouble gaining and keeping close, loving relationships because they come off as being less than genuine.

Typically, however, an inflated self-esteem is generally a sign of the exact opposite. Most people like this are hiding their true selves and are actually riddled with low self-confidence. The false mask of bravado is not true self-esteem, and this confidence is really just a form of self-deception.

Understanding the Meaning of Self-Esteem

Self-esteem is defined as confidence in your own self-worth, a sense of self-respect. You are not respecting yourself if you do not believe you are worthy of respect and happiness, nor are you respecting yourself by hiding behind an inflated ego.

To truly find your own self-worth and build a true and balanced healthy self-esteem, you have to first be honest with yourself. Stop hiding behind fear or a false sense of confidence. Often, being honest with ourselves is harder than being honest with an outside person.

Self-esteem is truly a balancing act that everyone has to work on. To build a healthy and balanced self-esteem you must first and foremost be honest with yourself. Only then can you start to work on your view of the world as a whole and make real changes that could change your life for the better.

Self-Discovery Challenge:

List at least five things you are afraid to do (not things you are afraid of i.e. spiders, but things such as speaking in public or afraid to ask someone for a referral):

Of the five things listed above, what is the worst thing that could happen if you attempt them?

List one new thing you will do this week:

Chapter 2 - Confidence

"No one can make you feel inferior without your consent."
Eleanor Roosevelt

Lack of confidence can paralyze your life. It can prevent you from doing great things just because you don't believe in yourself and can turn you into your own enemy. Lack of confidence doesn't only have a devastating effect on your mind, but is also responsible for the way other people treat you.

If you are unable to develop the self-confidence you need every aspect of your life gets affected. It affects your education, employment, relationships and social situations. However, it's never too late to recognize this and start working to improve your self-confidence to achieve what you desire in life.

If you are able to understand the problems associated with the low level of your self-confidence, it will let you better understand the corrective steps you need to take in order to develop your self-confidence to reach higher levels. For example, if you suffer from shyness or fear it indicates a self-confidence problem. It is typical for people with low self-confidence to hide from interacting with others and avoid situations that call for such interactions. However, by making conscious efforts and using correct knowledge needed for rebuilding your self-confidence, you can gradually correct this situation.

Your mind and your emotions are the tools required for developing your self-confidence and they always remain with you. It's your mind that can eliminate negative emotions like fear and shyness and put you on a track on which you will continue for the rest of your life. First you need to see yourself in a positive light, only then will other people see you in the same way. When you have confidence in yourself you will earn the confidence of others and command their respect. Mostly our thoughts are responsible for low self-confidence. The right way to tackle this problem is to win over negative thoughts with positive thinking. This is a sure method for building and governing your self-confidence. Positive thinking is how you can develop yourself into a much stronger and confident individual.

Negative thoughts invariably lead to negative or even unlawful actions whereas positive thinking leads to positive actions. Your positive actions will lead to more positive thinking and result in more positive outcomes. Both positive and negative thinking are ongoing behavioral patterns. But when you are able to develop a positive mindset, you exude confidence and are well on your way to success. The key to developing your self-confidence is to start small. If you begin by doing big things to develop your self-confidence and fail, it can have a big negative outcome. So take small steps in the beginning so that even if you fall your self-confidence isn't damaged.

Don't make the mistake of developing your self-confidence by yourself. Surround yourself with people who support you and will provide encouragement when things get tough and you start feeling low. Although it's good to have more people on your team, even if you have just one person other than you, you know you have someone who will encourage and support you.

And finally, never quit your efforts even if the results are slow in coming. Just take a firm decision that you will not quit until you develop your self-confidence to the levels you desire - no matter how tough things get or how long it takes.

Learn to Let Go and Build Back Your Confidence

Many of us are experiencing "the calm before the storm". We are under the impression that the present is just a hoax and that our life is yet to begin. We believe that all we had until today were false starts. And, when the world sees us half the way, we firmly assert that we are at the starting blocks.

The rate at which change is happening in this world, one is led to believe that change is that one sudden, spectacular and irreversible event that everyone takes note of. The need is for us to realize that, as always, change is still a gradual forward movement and involves a lot of "on" and "off" days. We give into peer pressure to make change happen and enter a vicious cycle of depression when nothing goes our way.

We need to stop pondering over the bad days and failures that are few but noticeable and set our eyes on our successes that are gradual and unnoticeable immediately to the eyes. We need to "let go" of the paralyzing power of failure. That involves understanding and implementing the need to change. On many occasions we resist change since it can be painful and filled with a lot of uncertainties. We experience a false sense of security by being static and not taking risks that we know may be necessary.

If a child learning to walk decides it's better to sit than take the risk of falling down the stairs or in the hallway while walking, he may never walk his entire life. Similarly, we need to look at failures as our baby steps towards the objective of building a life. Putting behind us the memories and sure signs of failure may not be easy.

"Letting go" may require us to set short term goals, which may seem to take us in an entirely new direction. We may be apprehensive of losing sight of our goal and resist such a change. We must realize that every goal achieved, whether short or long term, is a step towards boosting our confidence and will add up to the achievement of our objective.

Sometimes, incorporating change may make us appear as inconsistent and unsure of our goals. One example may be that of Warren Buffett, who began his business as a newspaper boy and ended up as an investment banker, all the while, unnoticed by the media or business analysts. Developing confidence doesn't have a straight and simple formula to be implemented.

One of the best examples of letting go of the worst events is that of the stock market. The analysis of the daily gains made will show a rather irregular way of growth, while the bigger picture displays a definite and prominent growth over a decade or more. Similarly, we need to look at "off" days as just a passing phenomenon compared to the long stay of slow but steady progress. In our endeavor to achieve progress let us remember progress can "bottom-out" but it has no "top-up".

Changing Self-Talk

Self-confidence is one's belief in oneself. It refers to one's confidence in his actions, beliefs and competencies. Having self-confidence is the key towards a successful and fulfilling life. Self-talk can be described as that little voice inside your head which can either be beneficial or detrimental to your self-confidence. This inner voice usually critiques, give comments, or praises one's deeds and actions.

There are different views about self-talk in relation to building self-confidence. Some people may associate self-talk to the obstacles towards attaining true confidence in oneself. This can be true in the cases of people who have no drive to take the pessimism out of their heads. This can later become a vicious cycle where a person is perpetually trapped in a downward spiral of self-esteem decline.

There is also a school of thought which believes that self-talk is an important tool in developing self-confidence. The inner voice can be seen as a teacher, a mentor, or critic who gives constructive comments or a friend. Self-talk has been employed by successful people in their careers and in popular fields such as sports and show business.

Here are some few helpful tips on how to utilize self-talk towards developing a healthy self-confidence:

Listen to your inner voice: This is the first step in making good use of self-talk. Identify the inner voice in you and listen to what it's saying. Ask questions regarding the contents of the thoughts; the situations which brought about these thoughts; and the other factors which could have aggravated the situation. Remember that this is to be done under the general goal of building self-confidence, so try to be as honest as possible.

Thoughts Assessment: After the thoughts have been identified, it's time to assess them. What are these thoughts saying in general? What attitude towards the self is being projected by these thoughts? How have I responded to these kinds of thoughts in the past? What have these kinds of thoughts instilled in me throughout the years? Have they been helpful to me and my quest towards self-confidence? The general tone of the inner voice is as important as what its saying. Negative tones should be controlled and be reversed into positive ones.

Make a difference: Dealing with your inner voice can be a daunting task. If it's hard to talk to somebody who won't listen, it's even harder to talk and listen to yourself since there can be no sensible argument that could happen.

Getting rid of the negative thoughts inside your head will give the positive thoughts some space. It's all about rephrasing the negative thoughts to make them positive. Your concept of the world is based on your views of the world. You develop self-confidence by feeling good about yourself.

Self-Discovery Challenge:

List three negative thoughts (or self-talks) you currently have about yourself:

List three (or more) good qualities about yourself:

List three short-term goals you will achieve with your good qualities in the next month:

Chapter 3 - Relationship Building

"Indifference and neglect often do much more damage than outright dislike."
J.K. Rowling

While the majority of people can learn the nuts and bolts of relationship building, focusing on some basic techniques that can be learned is a must. The main ones, in no particular order, are:

Read: "Read" people well.
Rapport: Develop rapport with others.
Finesse: Have finesse; i.e. handle conversations and activities in a cordial manner.
Conflict Resolution: Resolve negative issues and conflicts without too much friction.
Support Co-Op: Gain the support and cooperation in working towards a common goal.

Reading People: All about Body Language

Body language is the meaning behind the words or the "unspoken" language. Surprisingly, studies show that only up to an estimated 10 percent of our communication is verbal. The majority of the rest of communication is unspoken. This unspoken language isn't rocket science. However, there are some generalizations or basic clarifications that can be applied to help with the understanding or translating of these unspoken meanings. Here are some basics below:

Smile – People like warm smiles. Think of a heartfelt warm-fuzzy, maybe your favorite pet, and smile.

Eyes - -If you don't look someone in the eyes while speaking, this can be interpreted as dishonesty or hiding something. Likewise, shifting eye movement or rapid changing of focus/direction can translate similarly. If more than one person is present in a group, look each person in the eye as you speak, slowly turning to face the next person and acknowledge him with eye contact. Continue on so that each person has felt your warm, trusting glance. Some suggest beginning with one person and moving clockwise around the group so that no one is missed, and so that you are not darting around, seemingly glaring at people.

Attention Span/Attitude – Other people can tell what type attitude you have by your attention span. If you quickly lose focus of the other person and what is being said, and if your attention span wanders, this shows through and makes you seem disinterested, bored, possibly even uncaring.

Attention Direction – If you sit or stand so that you are blocking another in the party, say someone is behind you, this can be interpreted as rude or thoughtless. So be sure to turn so that everyone is included in the conversation or angle of view, or turn gently, at ease and slowly, while talking, so that everyone is incorporated, recognized and involved in the conversation. Again some suggest the clockwise movement when working a group.

Arms Folded/Legs Crossed– This can be seen as defensive or an end to the conversation. So have arms hang freely or hold a glass of water, a business card or note taking instruments while communicating with others. Be open with open arms. Note: If you need to cross legs, cross at your ankles and not your knees. Sitting tightly folded up says that you are closed to communications.

Head Shaking – This is fairly accurate. If people are shaking their heads while you speak, they are in agreement. If they are shaking, "no," disagreement reigns in their minds.

Space/Distance – On the whole, people like their own personal body space. Give people room and keep out of their space. Entering to close can be intrusive and viewed as aggressive.

Leaning – Sitting or standing, leaning is viewed as interest. In other words, an interested listener leans toward the speaker.

While you are with others, note how their bodies read. If a person suddenly folds his arms across his chest and begins shaking his head "no," you've probably lost him. Try taking a step back and picking up where the conversation began. It's all about strategic planning!

Developing Rapport

Now let's take a quick peak at the basics of developing rapport with others. In a nutshell, what it takes is to ask questions, have a positive open attitude, and encourage an open exchange of communication (both verbal and unspoken), listen to verbal and unspoken communications and share positive feedback. Here are a few details on each step:

Ask Questions – Building report is similar to interviewing someone for a job opening or it can be like a reporter seeking information for an article. Relax and get to know the other person with a goal of finding common ground or things of interest. You can begin by simply commenting on the other person's choice of attire, if in person, or about their profile, if online, and following up with related questions. For example, in person, you could compliment the other person on their color choice or maybe a pin, ring or other piece of jewelry, and ask where it came from. In online communications, you could compliment the other person's background, smile, or mention that the communication style seems relaxed and ask if he or she writes a lot. Then basically follow up, steering clear of topics that could entice or cause arguing, while gradually leading the person to common ground you'd like to discuss.

Attitude – Have a positive attitude and leave social labels at home. Many people can tell instantly if you have a negative attitude or if you feel superior. So treat other people as you would like to be treated. And give each person a chance.

Open Exchange – Do encourage others to share with you. Some people are shy, scared or inexperienced in communicating and welcome an opportunity to share. So invite an exchange with both body language and verbal communication. Face the other person with your arms open, eyes looking into theirs gently (not glaring or staring), and encourage a conversation with a warm smile.

Listen – Be an active listener. Don't focus your thoughts on what YOU will say next. Listen to what the other person is saying and take your clues from there, while also noting the body language. For example, if the other person folds his arms and sounds upset, you may need to change the subject or let him have some space and distance; maybe even try approaching him later on and excusing yourself to go make a phone call. On the other hand, if the other person is leaning towards you, following your every word and communicating with you as if you are old friends, YES! You've built rapport!

Share – People like compliments, so hand them out freely without over doing it. Leaving a nice part of "you" is like a compliment. This will leave a good memory for the other person to recall - numerous times. That's good rapport. But do be sincere. False compliments aren't easily disguised.

Fundamentals of Finesse

Basically using finesse in handling relationships means using subtle skill, tact or diplomacy when handling a situation. This doesn't mean you need to use fancy, flowery phrases or lengthy 10-letter words. It means focusing on the positive in a friendly way, and not embarrassing the other person.

For instance, finesse means not telling a host that he or she has offended you or that his or her house looks or smells strange. Instead, it means politely excusing yourself upon entering, and informing the host of an unplanned meeting that came up or family member who dropped by unexpectedly, and that you wanted to drop by for a quick "Hello" to thank the host for the invitation. Keep things simple here, smile and be on your way without causing hard feelings.

Conflict Resolution

Conflict is a normal part of any healthy relationship. After all, two people can't be expected to agree on everything, all the time. Learning how to deal with conflict—rather than avoiding it—is crucial. When conflict is mismanaged, it can cause great harm to a relationship, but when handled in a respectful, positive way, conflict provides an opportunity to strengthen the bond between two people. By learning these skills for conflict resolution, you can keep your personal and professional relationships strong and growing. How do you handle conflict?

Conflict arises from differences, both large and small. It occurs whenever people disagree over their values, motivations, perceptions, ideas, or desires. Sometimes these differences appear trivial, but when a conflict triggers strong feelings, a deep personal need is often at the core of the problem. These needs can be a need to feel safe and secure, a need to feel respected and valued, or a need for greater closeness and intimacy.

Managing and resolving conflict requires the ability to quickly reduce stress and bring your emotions into balance. You can ensure that the process is as positive as possible by sticking to the following guidelines:

1. Listen for what is felt as well as said. When we listen we connect more deeply to our own needs and emotions, and to those of other people. Listening also strengthens us, informs us, and makes it easier for others to hear us when it's our turn to speak.

2. Make conflict resolution the priority rather than winning or "being right." Maintaining and strengthening the relationship, rather than "winning" the argument, should always be your first priority. Be respectful of the other person and her viewpoint.

3. Focus on the present. If you're holding on to grudges based on past resentments, your ability to see the reality of the current situation will be impaired. Rather than looking to the past and assigning blame, focus on what you can do in the here-and-now to solve the problem.

4. Pick your battles. Conflicts can be draining, so it's important to consider whether the issue is really worthy of your time and energy. Maybe you don't want to surrender a parking space if you've been circling for 15 minutes, but if there are dozens of empty spots, arguing over a single space isn't worth it.

5. Always be willing to forgive. Resolving conflict is impossible if you're unwilling or unable to forgive. Resolution lies in releasing the urge to punish, which can never compensate for our losses and only adds to our injury by further depleting and draining our lives.

6. Know when to let something go. If you can't come to an agreement, agree to disagree. It takes two people to keep an argument going.

If a conflict is going nowhere, you can choose to disengage and move on.

Support and Cooperation

Relationships may begin with just two people, but more people eventually become involved. Work friends and associates, family members, old school friends and various other assorted persons interact daily, so gaining the support and cooperation in working towards a common goal is a plus in relationship building.

Cooperation is the process of working together to the same end. It is assistance, especially by ready compliance with requests. Support is "give assistance to; enable to function or to act."

How do we build trusting relationships through support and cooperation?

1. Show openness and be transparent: Share what you know, but also be willing to admit what you don't know.
2. Honor your promises: Do what you say you are going to do.
3. Speak your feelings: Don't just focus on facts, inject how you feel.
4. Volunteer information: Don't hold back information or make people pull information from you.
5. Keep other people's secrets: Don't gossip.
6. Be objective/fair: Consider other people before taking action or making decisions.
7. Listen more than speak: Be other-centric.

If you desire more support and genuine cooperation in your relationships then you're ready to venture down these five paths. Ask yourself these questions and write down the answers when necessary.

Path 1 - INTENTION

Are you clear about your intentions? Do you know the difference between a strategy and an intention? Knowing this difference is essential. Without this you tend to get stuck wanting other people to agree with your strategies. This can leave people feeling closed and defensive. Even worse, being attached to one particular strategy dramatically limits your opportunities to be satisfied.

Path 2 - ALIGNMENT

Is everyone on the same page? Do you have a shared intention and want similar results? Establishing alignment is the second path to the power of "us." The fact is that our interdependence puts limits on how far we can get in achieving any result we want without cooperation.

Path 3 - NEGOTIATION

Will your plans take everyone's needs into consideration? Will you keep at it until everyone is satisfied? Understanding the difference between compromise and collaboration will play a big part in everyone's willingness and ability to stick with the process.

Path 4 - AGREEMENT

What's the plan? What needs to happen and who's willing to do the work to make it so? After everyone's had their say and acknowledge they've been heard, people often think they've made agreements. In reality they've only expressed vague understandings of what they want and how they would like that to happen.

Genuine cooperation relies on your ability to make clear, doable requests that lead to definite agreements. Powerful agreements are specific about who, what, when, where, why and how. They include a positive confirmation of each person's willingness to do their part.

Path 5 - ACCOUNTABILITY

Will your agreements continue to work for everyone and create the results you want? Without accountability you can't know. If you wait too long to find out they aren't working, you may already have built up dangerous levels of frustration, resentment, and resignation.

You create accountability by setting specific times to review how well your agreements are working and to discuss what changes might be needed.

In summary, by learning to use more of these "nuts and bolts" of relationship building, focusing on some of these basic techniques can help build and grow relationships. More can be learned about each technique by simply heading to the local library or typing in the technique into your favorite search engine.

Self-Discovery Challenge:
In building your relationships (Personal or Professional):

Do you have a clear INTENTION?

Are you in ALIGNMENT?

Do you need further NEGOTIATION?

Is it time to make new AGREEMENTS?

How will you ensure ongoing ACCOUNTABILITY?

If you are not getting enough of these foods in your daily diet, you should consider taking a multivitamin or a supplement. If you are suffering from stress, chances are that you may be deficient in vitamin B as well as Omega-3 acids. Consult a physician before taking over-the-counter supplements.

Exercise is also crucial to relieving stress. As a matter of fact, when you feel stress coming on, the best thing that you can do to avoid it is to go for a walk or exercise. Doing something physical can sometimes really work out the problem that you are having.

Cardio exercises are the best way to work out stress. These get your heart pumping and naturally raise the serotonin in your brain, putting you in a better mood. Stress can be very draining on your physical being and exercise can 'right the wrong' and get your body back into shape. Exercise also boosts the body's immune system, which also suffers under stress.

Get yourself into an exercise routine. Work out in the morning or after work doing cardio vascular exercises that will give both your mind and body a boost, as well as help control stress. In the evening, you can practice yoga or stretching exercises that can help tone your body and relax you.

Don't want to exercise? Do something physical. Cleaning the kitchen floor will not only relieve your stress, but will also get the floor really clean. Doing something physical such as cleaning, is one of the best stress relievers available. It works better than any pill, costs nothing and, when you are finished, you will have a really clean house!

Chapter 4 - Stress Management

"The big, bad unknown is only that until it is known. Then you look back and wonder what all the fuss and worry was about."
S.A. Tawks

Stress is an intrusion on your peaceful existence. All of us strive to have orderly and peaceful lives. We tend to develop well when we get into certain routines. Human beings are all animals. If you have ever owned a dog, you may have observed that the dog thrived very well on routine. You had to walk the animal a certain time each day, it had to be fed at a certain time each day, and it slept at a certain time each day. The dog depended on a routine.

When the routine was broken, the dog would do things such as have accidents in the house, or behave in another destructive type manner. This is because the dog was actually stressed out. Why was the dog stressed out? His or her routine had been broken.

Human beings behave the same way. Parents often find that their children will behave much better when they have a set routine than if everything is pandemonium in the household. Routines give a child a feeling of security, which is the one thing that a child wants most of all.

Many people will complain that their kids are unruly and don't want to go to bed on time. Their bedtime "routine" involves telling their kids to go to bed. It then escalates into screaming at their kids to go to bed, to threatening their kids with punishment if they don't go to bed.

The entire "go to bed" issue can be avoided if the parents simply set a bedtime routine. Milk and cookies or a bedtime story and being tucked in every night. The children know what to expect and actually end up looking forward to bedtime. This gives children an added sense of security, something that they really need in their lives.

We all want to feel safe and secure, but as we get older, we realize that we cannot always count on things being the same. We experience different incidents in our lives that turn our world upside down and cause us to feel stress. Most of these incidents we cannot control, others we can control to a certain degree. Some of us are fortunate enough not to experience these stressors until adulthood. Others experience stress as young children.

Stress can be pinned to an outside factor or something that we create in our own mind. If we are creating self-induced stress, chances are that something from the outside triggered this condition and the resulting response.

Some of the more notorious causes of stress are:

Death of a loved one: This can be a spouse, parent, child or friend. Death is part of life, but the death of a loved one is something that causes significant stress. Our hearts are broken as we grieve for our loved one and our lives are seriously disrupted. This is something which we can do little about, unfortunately, and also something we all have to deal with, sooner or later. Many people recover from this stressor and continue with their lives. Others never fully recover. Death of a loved one can cause a number of serious illnesses that we take on ourselves, including depression.

The death of a child is probably the worst pain anyone can endure and many people never fully recover from this type of stress, however, they do manage to go on with their lives for the sake of others around them. Despite the fact that the death of a child is enough to put anyone over the edge, most people have more of a life force and feel compelled to go on. However, this is one stress factor that can be completely devastating to someone emotionally and most never fully recovers.

Divorce: Not all of us are glad to get rid of our ex-spouse. Divorce is a major stressor in our lives. In addition to causing us to feel stress, it can also stress out our children. Many couples are so wrapped up with their own emotions during a divorce they fail to notice the impact of the situation on their children. Chances are that the kids are feeling quite a bit of turmoil, even if they are too young to understand what is really going on. In fact, younger children can experience even more stress than older children in the case of their parent's divorce because they cannot put their emotions into words, nor can they understand that daddy or mommy going away has nothing to do with them. To a young child, everything in the world has something to do with them.

A child who experiences the trauma of his or her parents' divorce will feel stress. In some cases, the stress may manifest itself to a number of psychological disorders, including anxiety. The routine has been broken and the child no longer feels safe, so he or she will come up with a way to alleviate the stress and retain some sort of control over their lives by developing a physical disorder. Children should see a counselor when the parents' divorce, whether or not they appear "fine." Some children will be able to deflect the stress better than others, but it's always a good idea to make sure that the child truly is "fine."

Moving: Even if you are moving from a shack to a palace, this is still stressful. It may be a happy occasion, but it's still a disruption of your routine. Any disruption of your routine causes stress. Moving disrupts the entire family.

Let's face it, everyone hates moving. Packing up all of your belongings and then unpacking them is just a hassle. Very few of us are fortunate enough to be able to have someone do all of this for us so it tends to be stressful. However, even if we don't have to lift a finger, moving is still a disruption of our normal routine.

It will take a while before you can get established into your new home. Until you do, you should try to maintain as much of your normal routine as possible, especially if you have children.

Major Illness: Any type of major illness is a significant stressor for the entire family. One person being ill doesn't just affect that person, but everyone around him or her. A major illness is one of the worst stressors we can endure as it can go on for years, taking its emotional toll on everyone around, especially children.

Many people who experience a major illness enter into a depression. This is usually due to the dramatic change in their life. Others will most likely also enter into a state of depression or exhibit unusual behavior. A young person who has a very ill parent may start turning to drugs, alcohol or other behavior, to alleviate the stress he or she feels due to the parent's illness. They will be unable to deal with the stress and chances are that the rest of the family will be emotionally unavailable for help. Self-medicating with drugs, alcohol or even promiscuous sex is a way for some young people to cope with the illness of a parent.

Job Loss: In addition to being humiliating, the loss of a job will most likely throw you into financial turmoil. Losing a job often results in depression as well as anxiety. Not only did your self-esteem take a hit, but you are also worried about money. You will probably experience stress until you get a new job or reconcile yourself to the fact that you will have to get by on less money.

Until you get your bearings, you will face a disruption in your lifestyle as well as your financial status. The uncertainty that surrounds getting another job also affects us when it comes to stress. Losing a job is hard, but having to find another job can be just as difficult.

Even if we quit a job for a better job, this is still considered a stress factor. Starting a new job, while a good thing, is stressful for most individuals. Why? Because it breaks our routine, and again anything that breaks our routine causes stress.

These are just a few of the major stress factors that we, as a society, face. There are other things that can lead to stress, but these are among the worst.

In some cases, happy events such as the birth of a child, marriage, or even a new car can lead to stress. Even though these are joyous occasions, they are stressful. Why? They tend to disrupt our lifestyle.

Are you sensing any sort of pattern here with regard to stress? Each of the aforementioned stressors all has one thing in common - they disrupt our lives. We don't like to have our lives disrupted and when it happens, even if it a good disruption, it causes stress or uneasiness.

We cannot go through life like robots and expect for nothing to ever change. We are going to experience stressful situations throughout our lives. How we handle the stressful situations will determine how well we can manage stress. There are both good ways and bad ways to manage stress.

There are many ways that you can deal with stress that don't involve using drugs or alcohol. As a matter of fact, you are better off if you can avoid any type of prescription drug for your stress. Stress can be managed by many different natural methods.

The first thing that you need to do is to find out the cause of your stress. Once you have found the cause of your stress, you need to address this fact. The cause may be something that you can eliminate, or it can be something with which you have to live with.

In many cases, if stress is the result of something happening with your job, you have to ask yourself if the job is worth your health and the health of your entire family. Remember, when you suffer from stress, it often causes others to suffer from the same stress. If you are employed at a place where you are actually stressed out all the time, is it really worth it to continue in this employ? What sort of quality of life do you have if you hate what you have to do every single day?

Quality of life has significant value, or at least it should. There comes a point in everyone's life when they have to decide what is truly important. Remember that no one ever, on their death bed, lamented that they didn't work hard enough. Many of us end up not seeing the truly important aspects of life until it's too late.

If you can eliminate the stressor whether it's a personal relationship, a job, or even a certain situation, you will be all the happier for it in the long run. If a job or a person is really giving you that much stress, to the point that you have to seek professional help, is the person or situation worth it?

If the cause of your stress is something over which you have no control, you need to evaluate the problem, face it and seek help. There are many different counselling methods that incorporate behavior techniques to address stress. Medication can be useful in some situations, but tranquilizes should never be a long term "cure" for stress.

Natural cures for stress include behavior management techniques, proper diet and exercise, herbal remedies and yoga techniques. These will actually work towards alleviating your stress.

Behavior Therapy: Behavioral therapy is a psychological treatment option that modifies destructive behaviors by introducing appropriate behaviors. After initial treatment sessions to establish a relationship with the patient, a variety of techniques may be followed. A few of these options include:

- Modeling uses observation to learn a new behavior.
- Conditioning utilizes reinforcement to encourage or discourage a behavior.
- Flooding revolves around the technique of systematic desensitization. In flooding, patients are intentionally exposed to situations that cause their greatest anxiety in order to help them learn to overcome it.
- Systematic Desensitization is similar to flooding technique, but at a slower pace. The individual is exposed to the anxiety-causing

fear first in a role-playing session. After the person has become acclimated to the role-play, she is then exposed to the actual situation.

- Progressive Relaxation requires complete relaxation of the patient's body to relieve anxiety and stress. Once relaxed, this technique may be used to relieve existing stress, or to prepare the patient for a systematic desensitization session.

These are just a few of the behavioral therapy treatment options that are available to patients suffering from mental disorders, including stress and anxiety.

Massage Therapy: The demand for massage therapy has doubled in the past 10 years. This is largely due to the fact that massage therapy is so effective at relieving stress. Massage therapy is a licensed practice.

Massage is very useful helping with stress and particularly the symptoms of stress, which are tightened muscles, aches and pains. Massage therapy can work wonders on the stressed out body and also work to relieve your mind. It helps to shift your mind away from your worries and allows you to relax.

There are several different types of massage therapy that are available to people who are undergoing stress. They range from a traditional deep-tissue massage to a soft-tissue massage. In addition to relieving stress, massage therapy is also used to treat aches and pains resulting from exercise or sports injuries as well as a number of other ailments. A licensed massage therapist will be able to recommend the type of massage therapy for your particular situation.

Proper Diet and Exercise: Have you ever wondered why so many people are on medication for stress? What is it that is so different now than 30 years ago?

One of the major differences in our lives is the food we eat. Most Americans do not eat a healthy diet and more than a fair share are overweight. Many doctors believe that stress, and the onslaught of people suffering from depression, is due to a vitamin deficiency. The stress that many of us suffer from today may be the result of simply not eating a healthy diet.

We all know that proper nutrition is essential for a healthy body, but what about a healthy mind? We are hearing more about good nutrition for mental health as well as physical health.

Certain foods are natural mood enhancers. These include:

Dairy products - Dairy is usually high in protein and can improve a physical response to stress. Dairy is in milk or cheese, and by having dairy you can expect less physical problems due to stress as well as enjoying a lighter mood.

Fish - Fish that is rich in fatty acids, such as salmon, is good for the body as well as the mind. We all know that fish is considered "brain food," but fish that is high in Omega-3 fatty acids is a natural way to treat depression. There are studies that indicate that people who suffer from depression related to stress have low levels of Omega-3 fatty acids in their body.

Strawberries - These can keep your blood sugar levels stable, which can be another cause of stress. Strawberries are a natural way to stabilize your mood.

Spinach - Folic acid is essential to good health and spinach is high in this B vitamin. Studies have also indicated that people who have low levels of folic acid are more prone to depression. Folic acid increases serotonin naturally, which is exactly the way that medications to treat depression work on the brain.

Turkey - Turkey is another food that boosts the serotonin and contains Tryptophan, an amino acid that can actually make you calm. Remember how sleepy you felt after eating Thanksgiving dinner last year? That was from the Tryptophan, a natural tranquilizer.

Brazil Nuts - These contain selenium, which is another mood enhancer, however, too much of this can prove toxic for your system so eat these nuts sparingly, but include them in your diet.

Complex carbohydrates - These also contain tryptophan and, although we have been warned to "stay away from carbs" these past few years, we need complex carbs, not simple carbs. If you are watching your diet, stay away from simple carbohydrates, such as cakes, cookies and sweets, but eat complex carbs, such as sweet potatoes, that are rich in tryptophan.

Clams, Oysters, and Cottage Cheese all are high in Vitamin B12. Raw clams and oysters have been considered an aphrodisiac for a long time, but cottage cheese is also rich in this vitamin that has been known to enhance your mood and avoid stress.

Herbal Remedies: There are natural, homeopathic remedies used to treat stress. Some common herbal supplements for stress include:

Lemon balm: Several small studies have found that this supplement, which is part of the mint family, can improve mood and induce feelings of calmness.

Valerian root: This herb has been used to treat of anxiety and sleep disorders. Low doses on this herb are considered safe when taken for less than one month. High does may cause changes in heart rhythm and blurred vision.

Chamomile: This herb is considered a safe plant and has been used in many cultures for stomach ailments and as a mild sedative. Some studies, primarily using combinations of chamomile with other plants, show it may have health benefits. Chamomile is best known as an ingredient in herbal tea.

St. John's wort: This herb has been used to treat anxiety and stress for years. There is an indication that it's very effective in treating mild anxiety and depression as well as stress. It naturally releases serotonin and has both mood stabilizing and calming effects.

This is not to say that anyone who is suffering from stress and depression should not seek medical attention or take medication when necessary. In some cases, it is necessary to take prescription medications. However, a prescription should be used as a last resort, not the first thing that we try whenever we feel stressed.

Throughout our lives, we will encounter stress. We have to learn how to deal with it effectively or we will be doomed to taking medication just to get through everyday life.

If you are suffering from stress, try a natural herbal remedy before you embark on a series of medications or tranquilizers. If you plan to start using herbal supplements for stress, you should know that they can vary widely in their quality and content. For this reason, you should consult an integrative medicine practitioner or other expert familiar with these products before taking them.

Aromatherapy: Aromatherapy is yet another natural treatment for stress and involves the use of essential oils. Essential oils are derived from natural by-products such as tree bark, flowers, fruits or grasses. They are very concentrated and can be used either with an infuser, in which case the healing powers are inhaled into the lungs, or on the body as a massage oil, in which case the healing powers of the oil is absorbed into the bloodstream by way of the skin.

Essential oils are very concentrated and should never be used directly on the skin. Lavender is the one exception and is pretty much a cure-all for just about whatever ails you. Lavender oils are available at a variety of different places including online. In order for the aromatherapy to actually work, you have to use pure essential oils and not anything that is chemically produced.

Essential oils are not meant to be taken orally, but have been used as a treatment for a variety of minor ailments for thousands of years. Aromatherapy is particularly effective when combined with massage therapy. Most massage therapists incorporate aromatherapy into their practice, although this is something that you can easily do on your own. Simply get some lavender oil and an infuser and burn the oil so that you can inhale the scent. Not only will it relax and calm you, but it will also make the whole house smell fragrant.

Yoga and Meditation: These are Eastern arts just like aromatherapy and, like aromatherapy, have been around for thousands of years. People in the West tend to want to hurry everything along, which can be one reason why we are so much more stressed than people in the East. Yoga involves a series of stretching exercises that are designed to allow you to concentrate on something other than yourself. Meditation is the process of clearing your mind of negative thoughts and concentrating on nothing. Both are equally effective at calming you down if you understand how to use these techniques towards alleviating stress.

Yoga and meditation work pretty much the same way as exercising, cleaning and therapies do to relieve stress - they draw your attention away from the stressful situation and to something else. This is the secret to controlling your stress - to focus your attention on something that is either positive or neutral. Once you have learned how to use these different techniques to alleviate stress, you can then work on controlling how you react to stress.

The best way to treat stress over the long term is to identify the root cause of it, and see if your lifestyle can be changed to reduce it.

Self-Discovery Challenge:

What do you consider your stressors?

Of the stress-relieving steps listed in this chapter, what steps or measures can you take today to start relieving your stress? List as many alternate ways you will try.

What will you do if you start to feel the stress returning?

Chapter 5 - Goal Setting

"With ordinary talent and extraordinary perseverance, all things are attainable."
Thomas Fowell Buxton

The alarm rings, you wake up. You turn off the alarm and start the series of rituals that would get you showered, dressed, fed with breakfast, and eventually on your way to work. You kiss your spouse on the cheek as she readies herself for work and taking the kids to school. You say your goodbyes.

As you take your car from the driveway, you notice that all is quiet in the early dawn. You like to leave for work early to get away from the traffic. The trip is uneventful and the radio blares out music you have no fondness for.

As you arrive at work, you check your mail/email, and start work with a cup of coffee. Lunch comes and goes. You think about saving enough to run a small business in a few years. You have told yourself the same thing for three years now.

What's wrong with this picture? Is this you? Does the same dreary day pass by, one after the other, and you suddenly realize you're forty-five and feel you have little time left? Don't let this happen. Start setting goals with a timeline. Set goals by the SMART method.

The SMART method of setting goals has been around for a long time and has been used by many people. It's one of the many tools used by executives to hit their goals realistically and consistently with enough room to adjust to unforeseen circumstances.

Setting goals is a mind game that needs to be revisited as often as possible. This is to establish the goal consistently in the mind of the goal setter. Eventually the goal setter will have no need to be reminded on the goals he sets for himself.

SMART is an acronym for the following bywords:

Specific – The goal has to be as detailed as possible. This is to reduce the time to think about what the goal is. This must answer the basic questions of Who, What, When, Where, Which and Why. The more specific the goal, the more the end result can be envisioned by the goal setter. This dovetails into the sports theory that an athlete can see the goal before it is attained through training. Studies have affirmed that visualization helps immensely in the attainment of a desired goal.

Measurable – When setting goals, it must be specific that progress can be held up against a measure, or a benchmark. In bodybuilding, it is measurable to state that the goal is to bench press a weight of 200 pounds in two months' time. The old adage states: "if it can be measured, it can be attained" is also a known fact among athletes. Athletes keep a record of their performance, on and off the field of contest, in order to have something to compare against. They even measure other athletes in different sports to improve their understanding.

Attainable – This is a part where you determine the will to reach your goals. Do you think the goal is attainable? Will it help you fulfill your overall goal? The more specific a goal is, the more you can find ways of reaching your target. You develop and educate yourself on reaching those goals.

Realistic – Does it make logical sense? Getting to Mars and back within 20 days is a goal, but with the resources you have, is it realistic? Will it take a huge effort to achieve the objective? A person must be willing and especially able to achieve the goal. It is still realistic to aim high. It has to do with the rewards received, or the way the goal moves you forward. If you don't possess the skills or inclination to reach the goal, then the goals is unrealistic. No amount of motivation can get a man to do what he despises.

Time-bound – This is the most important of all. A goal has to have a deadline. This is to prevent the goal setter from letting his goal slide from one day to the next. The true price paid for goals is the time you give the goal. For example: "I will lose 10 pounds by January 1, 2016, which is three months from today."

Remember this: Time is the true price paid for your dreams. The earlier the dream can be achieved the more time you have to enjoy it. Don't let other people rob you of your goals, use the SMART method and share it with others so you can help each other reach your goals.

Self-Discovery Challenge:
Short-term goal

My short-term goal is:

It is important to me because:

Current factors impacting and/or relevant to the goal include:

My timeline is:

The strategies I've already implemented towards this goal include:

People (family, consultants, coworker, or friend) who can help me stay on track are:

Long-term goal

My long-term goal is:

It is important to me because:

Current factors impacting and/or relevant to the goal include:

My timeline is:

The strategies I've already implemented towards this goal include:

People (family, consultants, coworker, or friend) who can help me stay on track are:

Chapter 6 - Time Management

"Time is the most valuable coin in your life. You and you alone will determine how that coin will be spent. Be careful that you don't let other people spend it for you."

Carl Sandburg

Being able to manage your time is an important personal asset. Learning good time management skills takes time. Benjamin Franklin, one of the Founding Fathers of the United States, had twelve time management habits. Modern psychologists recognize three key elements in Franklin's three-hundred-year-old procedure for changing habits:

1. He started out committed to the new behavior.
2. He worked on only one habit at a time.
3. He put in place visual reminders.

You can use these habits in any order, but whatever you do, work on one each week. Although perfectionism is unattainable, you will see big improvements in your life.

Habit 1: Strive to be authentic.
Habit 2: Favor trusting relationships.
Habit 3: Maintain a lifestyle that will give you maximum energy.
Habit 4: Listen to your biorhythms and organize your day accordingly.
Habit 5: Set very few priorities and stick to them.
Habit 6: Turn down things that are inconsistent with your priorities.
Habit 7: Set aside time for focused effort. Make an appointment with yourself.

Habit 8: Always look for ways of doing things better and faster.

Habit 9: Build solid processes.

Habit 10: Spot trouble ahead and solve problems immediately.

Habit 11: Break your goals into small units of work, and think only about one unit at a time.

Habit 12: Finish what's important and stop doing what's no longer worthwhile.

Other tips to better manage your time:

-Get a grip on email. Try checking your email just three times a day. Train those around you to eliminate unnecessary emails and avoid "reply all."

-Limit meetings. Hold meetings only when necessary and keep them as brief as possible. Start on time, and people who are habitually late will quickly learn to show up on time.

-Use technology. There are apps to help you do everything faster, from scanning receipts to sharing contact information to taking notes and more.

-Delegate. Trying to do everything yourself is a common time-waster.

If you're constantly wishing there were more than 24 hours in a day, stop and ask yourself if you are correctly utilizing the time management tips above. Make sure to get enough rest and exercise. It sounds sense-less, but taking time out to exercise and get adequate sleep will give you the energy to get through the day more effectively and productively.

Self-Discovery Challenge:

What time management skills do you possess?

What time management skills do you need to work on?

Who can you enlist to help you with your time management skills?

Chapter 7 - Problem Solving

"We cannot solve our problems with the same level of thinking that created them."

Albert Einstein

You likely use problem solving every day. It is often taken for granted. People don't realize just how wonderful and important problem solving is. Most people don't even recognize it as a skill. In fact, most of the time problem solving is just second nature.

Problem solving can actually be defined as an art. The art of problem solving is something that we learn at a very young age. It helps us through life and is something we could not live without. Being able to solve problems is a life skill. It is important and it should be taken seriously to get the best results from it.

Looking at problem solving as an art can help you to become more appreciative of it. You can begin to use problem solving to its full potential and really respect that problem solving is important. You just need to learn more about problem solving as a skill and an art.

Problem solving is a fixture in life. You have to be able to solve problems. Problems pop up every day. Sometimes they are small and sometimes they are large. Sometimes solving a problem is a matter of life and death and other times it's merely a matter of keeping your sanity. Regardless of why you need problem solving, you cannot deny that you need it.

If you are a parent, then problem solving is a skill you no doubt could not live without. Children are full of problems and as the parent it is up to you to help them find the solution. Sometimes you have to be creative because problems that come up can sometimes be quite difficult to solve without a little creative thinking.

The same can be said in business. Businesses have plenty of problems and it's up to the employees to find a way to solve those problems. Again, sometimes simple problem solving techniques just are not going to work because some problems require more problem solving skills.

You run into problems every day, from flat tires to saving a failing product line. You are a problem solver and you probably don't even realize it. You should pay attention to your problem solving skills, though.

It is common for people to take problem solving for granted. We do it so much that it's not hard to believe that it becomes second nature. It is this familiarity with problem solving that leads us to take it for granted and to not be creative with our problem solving anymore.

If you think about how you solved problems when you were a child, chances are that you were much more creative then. Now you likely go straight to the "tried and true" methods instead of trying new things.

The problem with this, though, is that taking problem solving for granted can make you a lazy problem solver. You may no longer spend time trying to solve a problem but rather go to a "tried and true" solution. It may not be the best solution but since you are a lazy problem solver, you don't take the time to actually use your problem solving skills to try to come up with a better solution.

Problem solving can be an amazing process, but it's up to you to make it that way instead of just something you do because you have to. You have the ability to become a great problem solver, but you have to begin looking at it as an art.

The art of problem solving involves more than just jumping to the easiest solution. You have to really take time and analyze the problem. You have to come up with various solutions so you can find the perfect solution. You have to really make a conscious effort to solve a problem in a new way or the best way.

Here are some aspects of problem solving that you should start to use. You should take these aspects and apply them the next time you have a problem, no matter how big or small it is. You will then be able to understand the art of problem solving.

Be flexible. As mentioned, you have to go beyond your comfort zone. You have to avoid the immediate urge to go to the tried and true methods. You have to be flexible and willing to try something different. You will never know how great a solution may be if you don't try it.

Take time to think. You may need to step back and consider the situation before acting. You should brainstorm a little about the different ways you can solve this problem. Look at your options and think before taking action.

Ask questions. Part of solving a problem is to create new questions to answer. You may think this is silly and compounding a problem, but really by asking questions you will be led to deeper solutions.

Look at the problem in a different way. You cannot approach the problem as you normally would; try thinking differently about it. Avoid your natural tendencies. This may be hard at first but once you get used to thinking differently it will become second nature.

Think unconventionally. Come up with solutions that make no sense. You might surprise yourself and actually run across an unconventional idea that is the perfect solution to your problem.

By using these ideas you can begin to start looking at problem solving in a whole new way. You will no longer just jump to the obvious conclusion, but rather be able to really find the perfect solution. All it really involves is stepping back and taking some time. Not all problems must be solved right away. It is those problems that really let you put the art of problem solving to good use.

Problem solving involves many different skills. The most important skills are outlined below.

Use creative thinking. You have to be able to think in a creative manner and to see beyond the obvious if you ever want to be a good problem solver. You cannot just stick to the obvious, because in most cases, that will never get the problem solved. You have to be willing to think outside the box, brainstorm a little and come up with a unique solution. Creative thinking can make a person a perfect problem solver. Being able to think creatively allows a person to come up with solutions to problems that others may never even think about. A person is able to come up with good ideas that may not be so obvious. Creative thinking is something that can be a huge benefit to almost any profession because quick thinking is a great skill.

Reasoning - Reasoning has a place in problem solving, but it's important not to let your reasoning overtake your creativity. Reasoning comes in handy, though, because it will help you weed out the good ideas from the bad ones to come to the final solution.

Objectivity - You have to be objective when approaching a problem. You cannot have preconceived notions about how the situation will end or how you can fix the problem quickly. You have to come to a problem with an open mind and the ability to try different things to solve it.

Positive attitude - Your attitude can go a long way in your success as a problem solver. You have to be positive. If you approach a problem thinking that you will not be able to solve it, then chances are that you will not be able to. You have to think positive and believe in yourself.

These skills will go a long way towards helping you be a good problem solver. The skills listed above are some of the major things you need in order to be able to solve problems in a constructive manner.

If you have these skills then you may need to refine them. If you do not have these skills, then you need to work on them. If you are committed to becoming a good problem solver, you need to have these skills to help you.

You can build upon these skills in order to help you become an even better problem solver. There are also other skills not listed above that can assist you in being a good problem solver. You just need to identify what things you already know, or can do, that could possibly be put to good use when you are solving problems.

Take inventory of your skills. You will find that many things you may not exactly see as a skill are actually a very nice asset to your problem solving. Go through your skills and see how each skill you have can in some way benefit your ability to solve problems. Not everyone will solve problems in the same way. That is just part of what makes us each unique individuals. However, you can often learn from others and how they solve problems. They may use a technique that is new to you or something that really works and that you'd like to use. Watch how others solve problems and see what you can learn from them.

There are many methods of problem solving. You probably use one method and stick to it to solve every problem you encounter. This can be a bad thing. You should try out different methods because sometimes one method works better for a particular problem than another method. There are three main ways people solve problems:

Questions - Some people solve problems by asking questions. They look at the problem and ask 'what if' – what if I tried this or what if this happens? Through questioning they are able to see the possible outcomes. This allows them to come up with the best solution that seems to be the one that will work to solve the problem.

Develop a process - For the more organized individual or the more complex problem, it can sometimes help to develop a problem solving process. This usually involves analyzing the problem, proposing different solutions, testing the solutions and then finally, applying the chosen solution. It is a very structured way of solving a problem.

Brainstorming - For the more creative problem solver, there is the process of brainstorming. This involves just sitting down and coming up with numerous ways to solve the problem. Some ideas may be out there and that is fine. Using innovative thinking and being creative can help a person come up with an unconventional solution to a problem.

Being able to solve problems is a natural thing that we all are born with. It is actually how you approach problem solving that will help determine how good of a problem solver you are.

You should be willing to try different methods and different ways of problem solving. This will allow you to be able to come up with many options as a solution to your problem. You will then be more likely to come up with the perfect solution. You have to approach problems with an attitude that is positive. You have to believe you can solve the problem and not immediately think about how hard it's going to be. You have to believe in your abilities. Self-doubt can kill even the best problem solving efforts. If you never believe that you can solve a problem, then you probably will never be able to solve the problem.

Your mind is very powerful. You have probably been told before that whatever you put your mind to you can accomplish. Well, the same is true for what your mind is against. If you think that you cannot do something, then you will not be able to do it. It really is that simple. Your mind is that powerful. "Mind over matter" – this saying says it all.

You have to try different things and work towards a solution instead of just waiting for the solution to become clear. You have to work at problem solving, but at the same time you have to be creative with your problem solving.

Problems come in every shape and size. They can be small or they can be huge. You have to always be prepared because most often problems come unexpectedly. They will just appear and you have to deal with them.

You cannot avoid problems, so it's only logical to become a good problem solver. A good problem solver is going to be an asset. They are someone good to have around. Make yourself that problem solver. Be the person everyone loves to have around. Be the person who can look at a complex situation and come up with a solution. Don't be the person that runs away and says "I don't know" or "I can't do it." There is no room for negative words when it comes to problem solving. Always remember that. Don't give up or make excuses. Tackle problems and make the effort to solve them. Put your mind to it and you can be a great problem solver.

Put the art of problem solving to work in your life and you will be amazed at how well it works. Stop giving up. Stop passing problems onto others. Solve your problems and you will be glad you did.

Self-Discovery Challenge:

Of the problem solving aspects above (Being flexible, asking questions, taking time, etc.), on a scale of 1-10, with 1 being not at all and 10 being extremely proficient, what would you rate your problem solving ability?

What actions can you take to make your ability a 10 – and keep it a 10?

Are you asking yourself the right questions when trying to solve problems? What questions do you use regularly?

What new questions can you start asking?

Chapter 8 - Affirmations and Visualizations

"Belief consists in accepting the affirmations of the soul; unbelief, in denying them."

Ralph Waldo Emerson

Is it possible to work in the course of self-development by using visualizations and affirmations?

Yes, it's possible to use visuals and affirmatives to manipulate through self-development. Since self-development is a lengthy process, it is always nice to have our mental capacity and capabilities assisting us along the way.

It is vitally important that you can clearly visualize the reality you wish to create. The higher the detail of your visualization, the deeper the impact will be on your subconscious mind. It is important that you visualize every detail you possibly can, especially feelings, emotions, and sensory perceptions. What will it feel like to achieve success? Imagine it, amplify it, and imprint it on your mind. The results will amaze you.

As human beings, we are highly influenced by habit: habit of action, habit of thinking, and habit of belief. It is these habits which are the driving force in how we shape our reality. Visualization is a very powerful tool that will prepare your mind for success. The more you visualize that which you want – the more aligned your thoughts, beliefs and actions will be – and this will ensure you manifest the reality you desire.

Still, we need support and help from others. It is always nice to have friends that share similar qualities as yourself. It gives you inspiration, so you don't feel as if you are in this huge world all by yourself. Having people around you with parallel interests, differences and characteristics is part of self-development. This is because influences reflect on how we cultivate our skills and abilities.

We need to set goals and make plans for our life easier. Organization skills and other human developmental skills are required. We learn from the inner self. The inner self is our director, thus the one in charge that carries us through the self-development phase.

Most people don't recognize that naturally we all develop to certain levels. Since influences factor into our development, we see that it could create problems. Problems could develop, such as bad habits, behaviors, thinking and so forth. This is often true when we associate with people that think negative and reflect their thinking on us. Our behaviors are persuaded by influences.

Visualizations and affirmatives can help you develop that higher plane of consciousness and self-awareness. You reap benefits, since while you are in the process of developing your skills, you will also build emotional competency. This process of development is highly essential, given that emotions for centuries have gotten many people in a world of trouble.

Since the world is changing toward technology, the Internet is encouraging young adults to go online and play games to build their visualization and affirmative skills. The games accessible have proven to assist some children with developing self-awareness while putting the emotions at ease.

If you struggle with the self-development process, perhaps you can join the online gamers and take advantage of the new age resolutions for self-development. Surely, you know however, that games are not the sole invention that we must use to navigate through the process of self-growth while using affirmation and visualizations.

In fact, it takes more than games to develop a single human being. What it takes is time, practice, preparation and willfulness. Time, preparation and practice in this order, collective with willingness, will encourage you to stay focused on the subject. You want to keep your goal in mind by using visualizations. We can find many benefits while working through our self-development in a logical order.

Affirmations are acknowledgments of the inner self, which gives one inspiration to move ahead. The affirmatives give us the aptitude to assert and defend our intentions. Affirmations help us to corroborate authentic messages that one can verify. Affirmatives are statements that come from our reports, speech, and so on. It allows us to build endorsement so that we can work toward our goals. For example, an affirmation might be "I'm a good problem solver and people always look to me for answers to their problems."

Visualizations are mental images that we conjure up in the mind. It gives us a clearer picture of what we are thinking, or what others are saying to us. When we develop mental pictures in our head it can give us new ideas, or help us develop new ideas. We create dreams through mental pictures, which also help us to develop new ideas.

Mental images are often created through brainstorming or meditation. When we brainstorm or meditate while conjuring up mental images, it inspires the mind. We develop plans, and design from this action. Moreover, we can take initiative action by picturing in our mind what we must do.

Visualizations help us to use thought to consider our beliefs, views, opinions, theories, concepts and so forth.

We can use visualization and affirmatives for developing the inner self. Self-development starts in the womb, and carries forward throughout the direction of one's life. We all have several ways to further visualization parallel to promoting our capability to employ affirmatives through meditation. Meditation can assist you with pulling your mind together to start visualizing the self in a scene of position, space and time. Meditation encourages relaxation, which helps you to stick to moderate plans while working through self-development. It will turn out to be easier for you.

Relaxation eases your mind, thus it helps you to take up again creating mental pictures in your mind so you can start thinking optimistically. We all must give the mind room to breathe so we can think positive in order to profit from visualizations and affirmatives.

Self-growth is a process that allows us to use affirmations and visualizations in order to manipulate through the procedures. Affirmatives and visualizations are encouraged in college and have been used to assist individuals with developing a positive mind. Positive thinking assists one with the process of self-development by giving courage. From beginning to end, mental pictures have been widely used as enforcers.

We all have to work our way through self-development. Despite where we pick up and move faster to develop our skills, we all have to get it done. Sadly, however, many people have left the world underdeveloped, and many more will leave the world the same way. Many people miss the benefits of meeting the inner self. The inner self is the entire being within each of us that sets us free from burden, distress, illness and other harms. We have the inner strength, which is the inner self that allows us to draw from its source, to find ways to develop the entire human being.

Yet, we have many things to consider. We have to discover our self-identity throughout the process of development. Online you will come across hints that will help you work through self-development by using affirmatives and visualizations. Many hints offered for self-development today are directed toward the new age arena. We are in the new age now, so why not explore the market to see what is happening. Take the tips and use them to your advantage.

We have the best of both worlds with affirmations and visualizations, since the two tools can help us reach out above our limits and go beyond our future. Using these tools, we can build on our future by applying the positive learning from our mental creations.

Self-Discovery Challenge: (Do this on a separate piece of paper)

Writing an affirmation letter can assist in generating the focus and details needed to create a new reality. You can use letters or just one or two sentences. The key to affirmations is to repeat, repeat and repeat.

Write down what your ideal day would look like from sunrise to sunset.

Write a letter to yourself explaining why it has been hard to achieve a goal. You might be very surprised about what comes out.

Write a letter to someone you admire about what qualities of theirs you would like to incorporate into your life.

What one or two sentence affirmation sticks with you that you will repeat each day to yourself? (For example: "I have total control over my visualizations;" or "I use the power of visualization to manifest the life I want;" or "My mind is focused and clear when I visualize.") Write your affirmation down below. Remember to post it everywhere you can see it and repeat it several times each day.

Chapter 9 - Mindfulness

"Be in the moment. Live in the moment."
Michele Sfakianos

Can You Embrace Mindfulness?

There is a lot of talk about mindfulness. What is mindfulness? Mindfulness is a state of active, open attention on the present. When you're mindful, you observe your thoughts and feelings from a distance, without judging them good or bad. Instead of letting life pass you by, mindfulness means living in the moment and awakening to the experience. Mindfulness is now being examined scientifically and has been found to be a key element in happiness.

It's a busy world. You wash dishes while keeping one eye on the kids and another on the television. You plan your day while listening to the radio and commuting to work, and then plan your weekend. But in the rush to accomplish necessary tasks, you may find yourself losing your connection with the present moment—missing out on what you're doing and how you're feeling. Did you notice whether you felt well-rested this morning or that roses are in bloom along your route to work?

What can mindfulness do for you?

1. Increasing your capacity for mindfulness supports many attitudes that contribute to a satisfied life.

2. Being mindful makes it easier to savor the pleasures in life as they occur, helps you become fully engaged in activities, and creates a greater capacity to deal with adverse events.

3. By focusing on the here and now, many people who practice mindfulness find that they are less likely to get caught up in worries about the future or regrets over the past; are less preoccupied with concerns about success and self-esteem; and are better able to form deep connections with others.

What can mindfulness do for your health?

-Helps relieve stress
-Reduces heart disease
-Lowers blood pressure
-Reduces chronic pain
-Improves sleep
-Alleviates digestive difficulties
-Prevent or reduce the effects of depression
-Prevent or reduce substance abuse
-Prevent or reduce eating disorders
-Reduces couples' conflicts
-Prevent or reduce anxiety disorders
-Prevent or reduce obsessive-compulsive disorder

Some experts believe that mindfulness works, in part, by helping people to accept their experiences—including painful emotions—rather than react to them with aversion and avoidance.

How do you practice mindfulness? There is more than one way to practice mindfulness, but the goal of any mindfulness technique is to achieve a state of alert, focused relaxation by deliberately paying attention to thoughts and sensations without judgment. This allows the mind to refocus on the present moment. All mindfulness techniques are a form of meditation, such as:

Basic mindfulness meditation – Sit quietly and focus on your natural breathing or on a word or "phrase" that you repeat silently. Allow thoughts to come and go without judgment and always return to your focus on breath or phrase.

Through body sensations – Notice subtle body sensations such as an itch or tingling without judgment and let them pass. Notice each part of your body in succession from head to toe.

Sensory – Notice sights, sounds, smells, tastes, and touches. Name them "sight," "sound," "smell," "taste," or "touch" without judgment and let them go.

Emotions – Allow emotions to be present without judgment. Practice a steady and relaxed naming of emotions: "joy," "anger," or "frustration." Accept the presence of the emotions without judgment and let them go.

Urge surfing – Cope with cravings (for addictive substances or behaviors) and allow them to pass. Notice how your body feels as the craving enters. Replace the wish for the craving to go away with the certain knowledge that it will subside.

A less formal approach to mindfulness can also help you to stay in the present and fully participate in your life. You can choose any task or moment to practice informal mindfulness, whether you are eating, showering, walking, touching a partner, or playing with a child or grandchild. Attending to these points will help you start by bringing your attention to the sensations in your body.

1. Breathe in through your nose, allowing the air to fill your lungs. Hold your breath for a few seconds. Now breathe out through your mouth. Notice the sensations of each inhalation and exhalation.

2. Now proceed with the task at hand slowly and with full deliberation.

3. Engage your senses fully. Notice each sight, touch, smell and sound so that you savor every sensation.

When you notice that your mind has wandered from the task at hand, gently bring your attention back to the sensations of the moment. Be in the moment. Live in the moment.

Self-Discovery Challenge:

Am I doing what I love and getting better at it each day?

What will I do today that will matter one year from now?

How am I moving things forward today?

Am I practicing mindfulness? If so how? If not, why?

What isn't working and what steps will I take to change it?

Conclusion

When it comes to trying to find the answers inside yourself, you have to dig deep into your soul and your mind to find the right answers you are looking for. It is a long process and no one will tell you that it's easy, yet you can accomplish much by putting forth effort. To get started, you have to be able to take a long look inside yourself, which is not easy for anyone, but in order to be able to find answers it has to be done. This is where a professional coach can help you.

A professional life coach helps you to search your mind and insight to help you find your hopes and dreams, as well as to feel motivated enough to make your wishes come true. This is all about finding yourself and helping you to have better insight of yourself.

It takes some time to become someone in a professional stance but as you grow, you will find that it will be easier for you to handle your responsibilities. This will help you to be able to define who you are and what you want in life. The process will help you to become a successful businessperson, as well as a successful individual. In order to become a professional you have to work at it. This is not going to be something that doesn't take any time or effort; this is going to be an ongoing effort.

People will experience hard times, but you will learn how to overcome this and walk through it. You will not only cross over discrepancy, but you will come across many self-emotions and experience the power of self-growth. You will feel anxiety, fear, resentment, guilt and a lot of uneasiness. However, when you are feeling this way, the professional coach will help you to learn to overcome it and move forward.

How does one get on the right path? It will all depend on you and your mind frame, on how fast you will progress. It is going to take some time but as you learn to work on it, it will come to you faster than someone who only thinks they want it. The coaching process will help you to go deep inside of your thoughts and feelings. Throughout the process you will create goals, both short term and long term. These goals, once down on paper, become real. You will place these goals in front of you so can see them and read them each day to keep your mind fresh. The more you see and read something the more it will become "real." In order to become the successful person you want to be, there is work that you are going to have to do.

When it comes to trying to find yourself, you are going to have to take a trip. This trip can be anywhere you want it to be. For some of us we have to go to our local library and others will stay home and search on the computer. How is the computer going to help us? There is information of all kinds on the internet that will help you when it comes to trying to develop your professional skill to become someone success-ful. Take an online class, or webinar, or just browse articles of interest to you.

If you feel you aren't ready for a coach, begin your self-development through studying and reading at the library, or a quiet place in your home, so that you have a peaceful environment for learning. There should be no noise to get us sidetracked while we are working.

Find your way to professional growth through your self-insight. Find your solutions. Just "Take Action Today!"

Self-Discovery Challenge:

List five ways you want to challenge yourself:

Of the five things you listed above, list some of the action items you will take to achieve these challenges:

What is one action you will take today to build a better future?

Resources

Twelve Time Management Habits by Benjamin Franklin, one of the Founding Fathers of the United States [World Wide Web]

www.fda.gov/food - This website contains lots of information on food handling, food storage, food spoilage and other food related issues.

www.takeactionwithmichele.com – My website is dedicated to personal growth, coaching, speaking and training for individuals and families in areas such as Leadership, Parenting, Communication, Personal Growth, Finances, and more.

www.youtube.com – This website contains "hands on" video demos for many of the instructional items in this book.

Index

About the Author

MICHELE SFAKIANOS (Sfa-can-iss) is a Registered Nurse, Certified Personal Coach, Speaker and Trainer. She is also a Leading Authority on Life Skills and Parenting, and an Award Winning Author. In 1982, she received her AS Degree in Business Data Processing/Computer Programming. In 1993, she received her Associate in Science degree in Nursing from St. Petersburg Junior College, graduating with Honors. In 1999, Michele received her Bachelor of Science degree in Nursing from Florida International University, graduating with High Honors. Michele received her John Maxwell Certification in Coaching, Speaking and Training in 2015.

Michele is the owner of Take Action with Michele, Inc. and is also the owner of Open Pages Publishing, LLC. Her first book "Useful Information for Everyday Living" was published October 2010 and was later changed to "The 4–1–1 on Life Skills" and released June 2011. Her other books include: "The 4–1–1 on Step Parenting," released October 2011; "The 4–1–1 on Surviving Teenhood," released October 2012; "Parenting with an Edge," released June 2013; and "Teen Success: It's All About You! Your Choices – Your Life," released June 2013. Michele has also written two children's books: Aaron's Special Family and Aaron Bug.

www.ingramcontent.com/pod-product-compliance
Lightning Source LLC
Chambersburg PA
CBHW060136050426
42448CB00010B/2150